Hal Leonard Student Piano Library

Piano Lessons
Book 1

Authors
Barbara Kreader, Fred Kern, Phillip Keveren, Mona Rejino

Consultants
Tony Caramia, Bruce Berr, Richard Rejino

Editor	*Illustrator*
Anne Wester	Fred Bell

To access audio, visit:
www.halleonard.com/mylibrary

Enter Code
2699-8397-3595-2659

ISBN 978-0-634-03118-2

Visit Hal Leonard Online at
www.halleonard.com

FOREWORD

When music excites our interest and imagination, we eagerly put our hearts into learning it. The music in the **Hal Leonard Student Piano Library** encourages practice, progress, confidence, and best of all – success! Over 1,000 students and teachers in a nationwide test market responded with enthusiasm to the:

- variety of styles and moods
- natural rhythmic flow, singable melodies and lyrics
- "best ever" teacher accompaniments
- improvisations integrated throughout the **Lesson Books**
- orchestrated accompaniments included in audio and MIDI formats.

When new concepts have an immediate application to the music, the effort it takes to learn these skills seems worth it. Test market teachers and students were especially excited about the:

- "realistic" pacing that challenges without overwhelming
- clear and concise presentation of concepts that allows room for a teacher's individual approach
- uncluttered page layout that keeps the focus on the music.

In addition, the **Piano Practice Games** books present basic theory, technique and creativity in ways that relate directly to the music in the **Lesson Books**. The **Piano Solos** series reinforces concepts with challenging performance repertoire.

The **Hal Leonard Student Piano Library** is the result of the efforts of many individuals. We extend our gratitude to all the teachers, students and colleagues who shared their energy and creative input. May this method guide your learning as you bring this music to life.

Best wishes,

Barbara Kreader   Fred Kern   Phillip Keveren   Mona Rejino

World headquarters, contact:
Hal Leonard
7777 West Bluemound Road
Milwaukee, WI 53213
Email: info@halleonard.com

In Europe, contact:
Hal Leonard Europe Limited
1 Red Place
London, W1K 6PL
Email: info@halleonardeurope.com

In Australia, contact:
Hal Leonard Australia Pty. Ltd.
4 Lentara Court
Cheltenham, Victoria, 3192 Australia
Email: info@halleonard.com.au

CONTENTS

* Students can check pieces as they play them.

SITTING AT THE PIANO

Ask yourself:

Am I sitting tall but staying relaxed?

Are my wrists and elbows level with the keys of the piano?

HAND POSITION

1) Let your arms hang relaxed at your sides. Notice how your hands stay gently curved.

2) Keep your hands relaxed and curved as you raise them to the piano keyboard.

3) When you are playing the piano, keep your fingers in this relaxed, curved position.

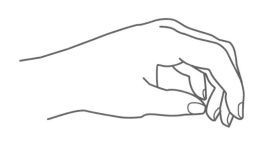

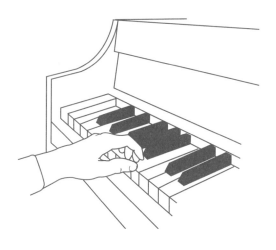

Feel The Beat!

Become aware of the heartbeat inside your body. Feel how it beats in an even pulse. Sometimes your heart beats fast, like when you run; sometimes it beats slowly, like when you are asleep, but it always beats evenly.

Rhythm In Music

Music has a pulse, too. Just like your heartbeat, musical pulse can go fast or slow.

Clap this pulse as your teacher plays the accompaniment below three different times at different speeds:

1) at a slow speed, 2) at a medium speed, 3) at a fast speed.

You can also play this pulse on the piano using any black key. Remember to keep the pulse even.

Accompaniments may also be played on the audio.

Accompaniment 1/2/3

4

Take A Look!

As you listen to the accompaniment below, stand and sing along with your teacher.

After the words "way down low," play on the **low black keys**. After the words "way up high," walk around your teacher and play on the **high black keys**.

1) When I look down low by my toe,
   Bugs and slugs and snails all grow.
   Way down low!

2) When I look up high in the sky,
   Birds and kites and planes fly by.
   Way up high!

Low ⟵

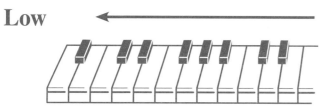

(Play the black keys way down low.)

High ⟶

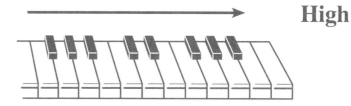

(Play the black keys way up high.)

Accompaniment

Steady (♩ = 145) 🔊 4

Kern, Keveren, Kreader

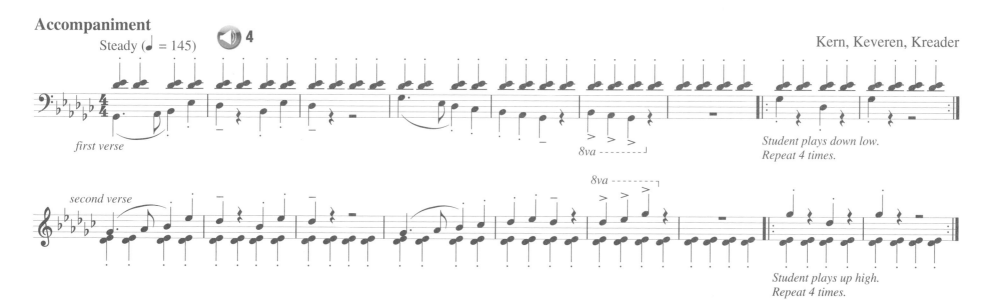

first verse

8va - - - - -

Student plays down low.
Repeat 4 times.

second verse

8va - - - - - - -

Student plays up high.
Repeat 4 times.

5

FINGER NUMBERS

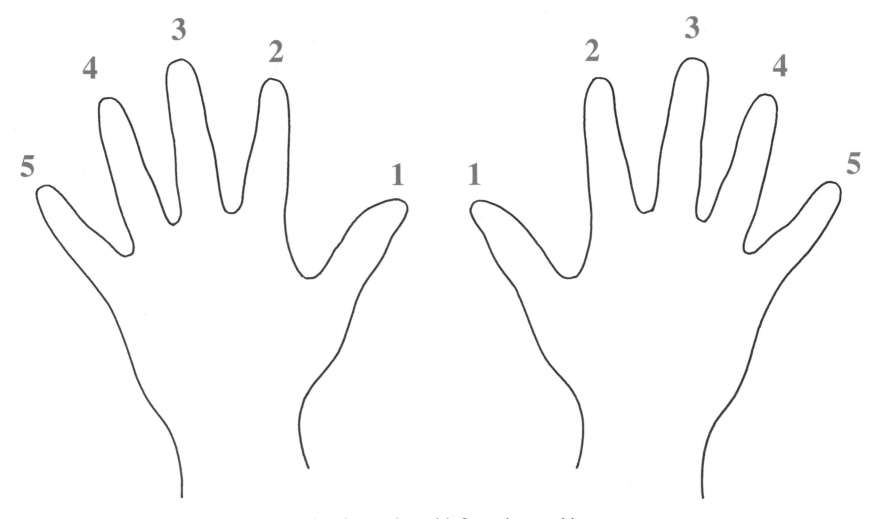

Place your hands together with fingertips touching.

Tap your 1st fingers (thumbs).
Tap your 2nd fingers.
Tap your 3rd fingers.
Tap your 4th fingers.
Tap your 5th fingers.

Tap 4s,   tap 2s,   tap 5s,   tap 1s,   tap 3s.

THE PIANO KEYBOARD

The piano keyboard is divided into sets
of two and three black keys.

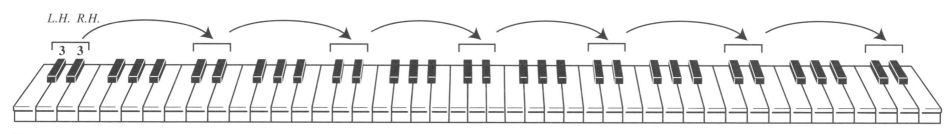

Low

High

TWO BLACK KEYS

Put your thumbs behind the first
joint of your third fingers and
use your third fingers to play the
groups of two black keys. Start
at the low end of the keyboard
and play higher.

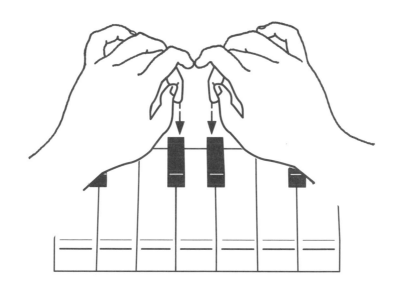

When you play the pieces
"Climbing Up" and "Climbing
Down" on pages 8 and 9, you
will play the groups of two
black keys as shown here.

Climbing Up

Two Black Keys
Moving Up The Keyboard

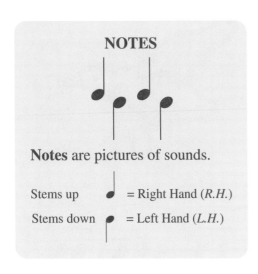
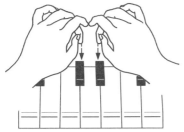

Play this song on two black keys with the third finger in each hand.

It is helpful to clap and sing the words of a piece before playing it. Remember to keep a steady pulse!

Climb - ing, climb - ing   up   this   tree,

R.H.

L.H.

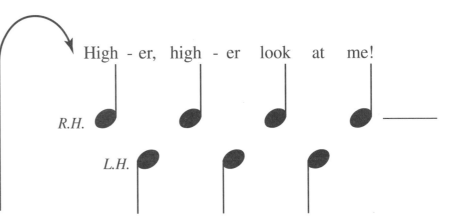

High - er, high - er   look   at   me!

R.H.

L.H.

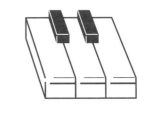

With accompaniment, student starts here: 🔊 **5/6**

With determination (♩ = 120)

mf

8va

8

Climbing Down

Two Black Keys
Moving Down The Keyboard

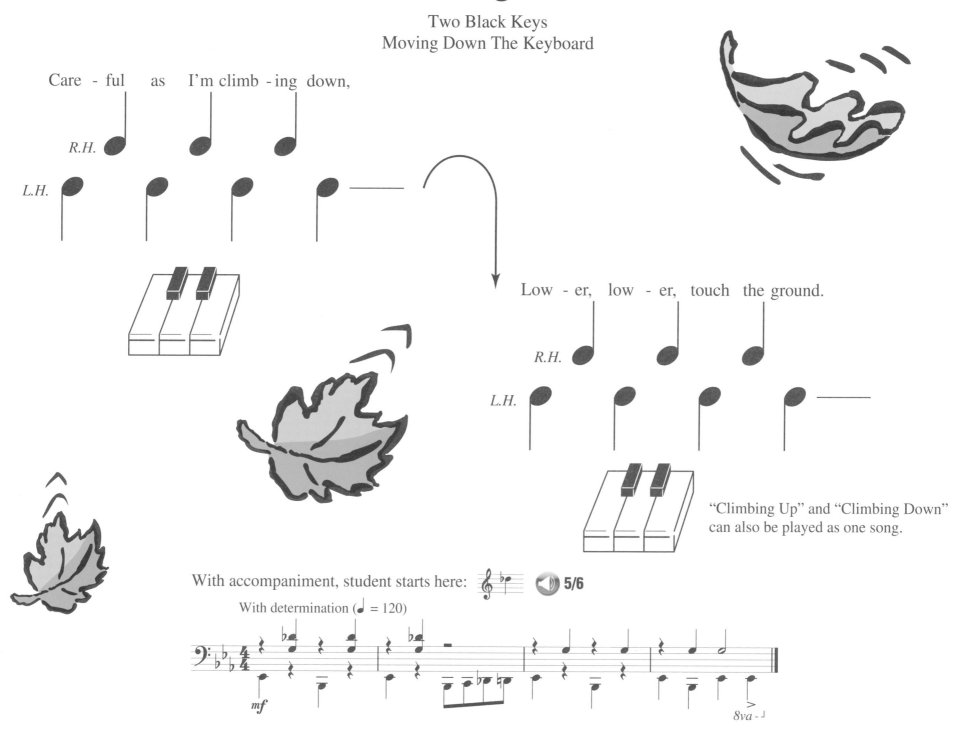

Care - ful   as   I'm climb -ing down,

R.H.

L.H.

Low - er, low - er, touch   the ground.

R.H.

L.H.

"Climbing Up" and "Climbing Down"
can also be played as one song.

With accompaniment, student starts here: 5/6

With determination (♩ = 120)

mf

8va -

9

My Own Song

With your right and left hands, choose any groups of two black keys in the upper part of the piano.

Listen and feel the pulse as your teacher plays the accompaniment below. When you are ready, play along and make up your own song.

Have fun!

Accompaniment

Flowing
(♩ = 100)

Repeat as necessary   *Last time*

THREE BLACK KEYS

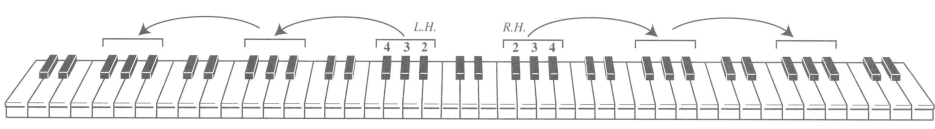

Low

High

Using your **left hand**, start in the middle of the keyboard and play the groups of three black keys with fingers 2-3-4 going **down the keyboard**.

Using your **right hand**, start in the middle of the keyboard and play the groups of three black keys with fingers 2-3-4 going **up the keyboard**.

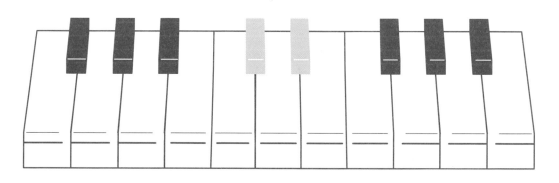

Play "My Own Song" again, using the groups of three black keys.

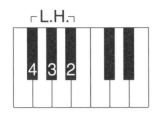

When you play these pieces by yourself, use the middle of the keyboard.

It is helpful to clap the rhythm of a piece before playing it.

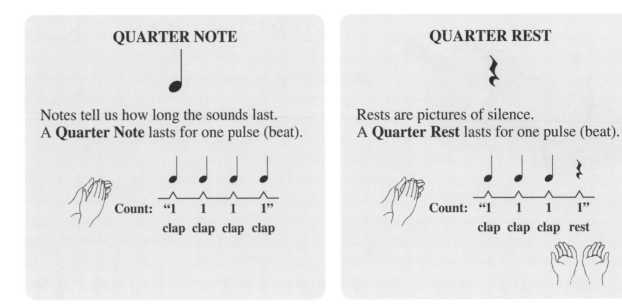

QUARTER NOTE

Notes tell us how long the sounds last.
A **Quarter Note** lasts for one pulse (beat).

Count: "1   1   1   1"
clap clap clap clap

QUARTER REST

Rests are pictures of silence.
A **Quarter Rest** lasts for one pulse (beat).

Count: "1   1   1   1"
clap clap clap rest

My Dog, Spike

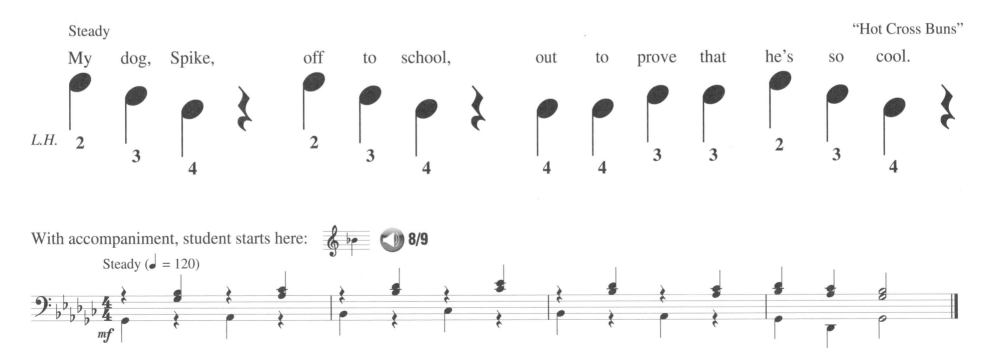

"Hot Cross Buns"

Steady

My dog, Spike, off to school, out to prove that he's so cool.

With accompaniment, student starts here: 8/9

Steady (♩ = 120)

12

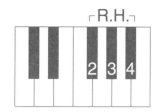

You can play "My Dog, Spike" and "Sorry, Spike" as one song.

Sorry, Spike

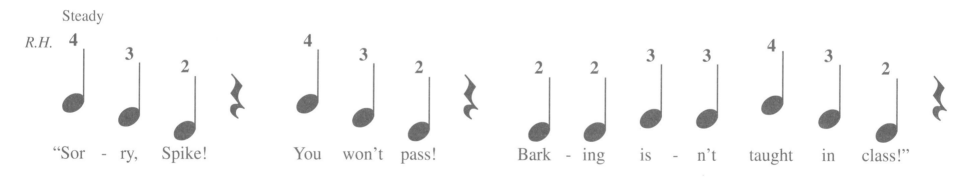

Steady

R.H.

"Sor - ry, Spike! You won't pass! Bark - ing is - n't taught in class!"

With accompaniment, student starts here: 🔊 **8/9**

Steady (♩ = 120)

mf

13

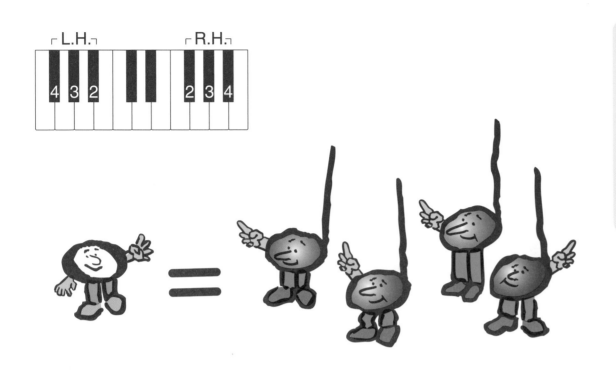

Merrily We're Off To School

Bouncy

"Mary Had A Little Lamb"

Mer - ri - ly   we're   off   to   school,   off   to   school,   off   to   school.

With accompaniment, student starts here: 10/11

Bouncy (♩ = 130)

mf

14

These small black boxes are called "clusters."
Play notes together using fingers indicated.

Here's our school bus. Honk! Honk! Honk! Hur - ry, it won't wait.

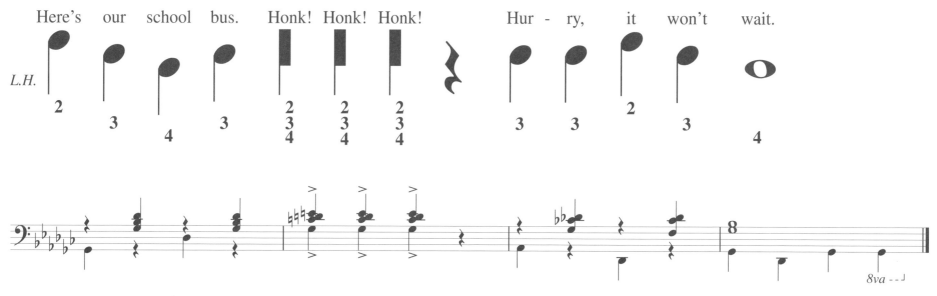

15

HALF NOTE

A **Half Note** fills the time of two quarter notes.

= 2 beats
= 2 beats

Count: "1   2"
clap - hold

My Best Friend

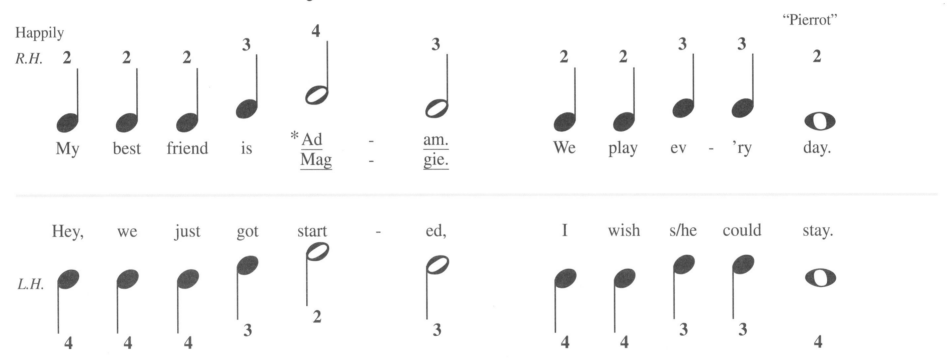

Happily

R.H.

My   best   friend   is   *Ad / Mag - am. / gie.   We   play   ev - 'ry   day.

"Pierrot"

Hey,   we   just   got   start - ed,   I   wish   s/he   could   stay.

L.H.

Play the first line of the song with your right hand; then play the second line of the song with your left hand.
*Fill in the name of your own friend.

With accompaniment, student starts here: 🔊 12/13

Happily
(♩ = 120)

mf

"So long!"

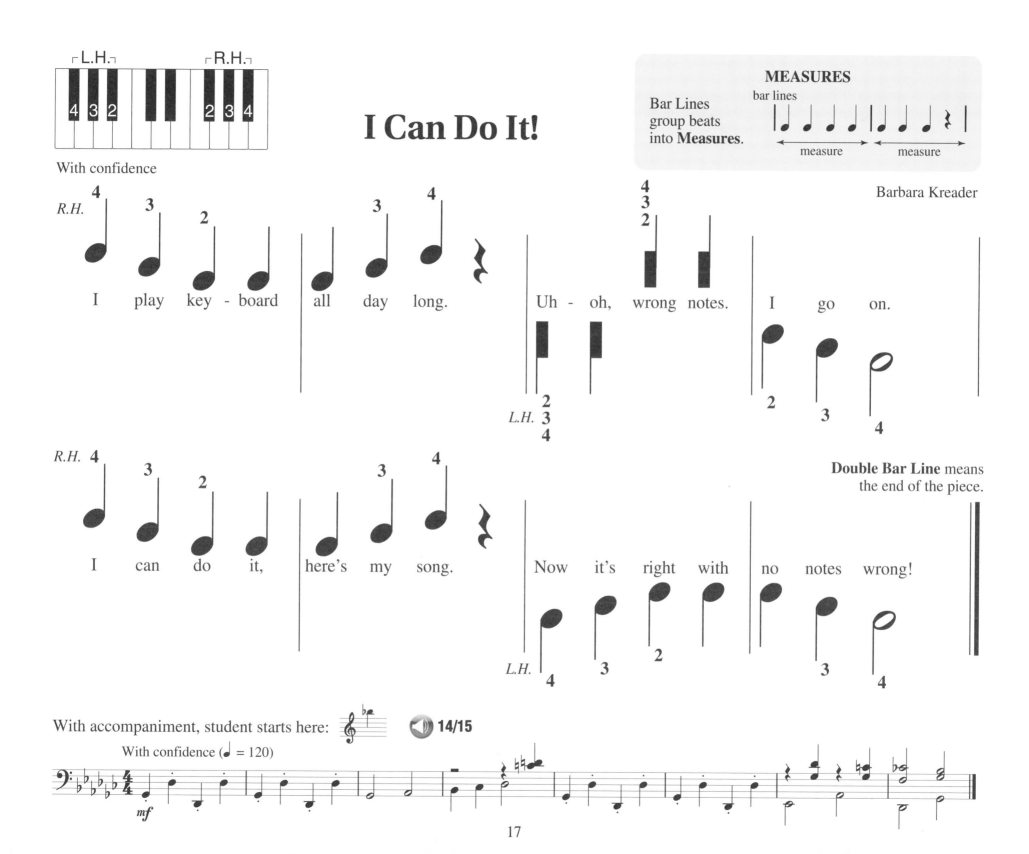

I Can Do It!

Barbara Kreader

With confidence

MEASURES

Bar Lines group beats into **Measures**.

Double Bar Line means the end of the piece.

I play key - board all day long. Uh - oh, wrong notes. I go on.

I can do it, here's my song. Now it's right with no notes wrong!

With accompaniment, student starts here:

With confidence (♩ = 120)

mf

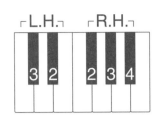

HALF REST

A **Half Rest** fills the time of two quarter rests.

= 2 beats

= 2 beats

Count: "1   2"
rest - rest

Let's Get Silly!

With excitement

Barbara Kreader

R.H.
4
Come play in the | yard with me; | laugh and twirl a - round.

L.H.
Tick - le all our | fun - ny bones; | fall down on the | ground.

With accompaniment, student starts here: 🔊 16/17

With excitement
(♩ = 130)

mf

18

8va

Make up jokes and | cra - zy names; | sing a fun - ny | song.

Laugh so hard that | we can't breathe. | Bring a friend a - | long.

19

Night Shadows

Quietly

Barbara Kreader

Shad - ows, shad - ows on the wall. My bear is scared and so am I.

But my night light's shin - ing. We can go to sleep.

With accompaniment, student starts here: 🔊 18/19

Quietly (♩ = 82)

p

With pedal

20

THE MUSICAL ALPHABET

Playing on the White Keys

Music uses the first seven letters of the alphabet. These letters are used over and over to name the white keys.

Alphabet Soup

With your right-hand third finger, play and sing the music alphabet three times, using this rhythm:

A B C D E F G

A B C D E F G A B C D E F G A B C D E F G A B C D E F G A B C D E F G A B C D E F G

Student part to be played by rote. 🔊 20

Fred Kern

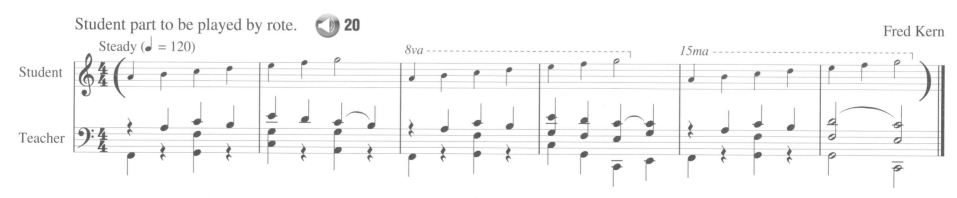

Steady (♩ = 120)

Student

Teacher

8va

15ma

21

C D E GROUPS

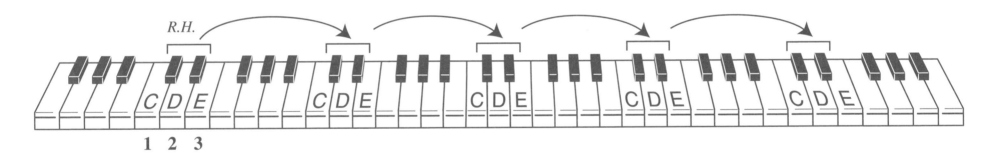

R.H.

C D E   1 2 3

With your right hand, start at the low end of the keyboard and play
the C D E groups with individual fingers 1-2-3 going up the keyboard.

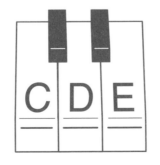

C D E

Now explore the keyboard,
playing the C D E groups
with your left hand using
fingers 3-2-1.

My Own Song
On C D E

With your right or left hand, choose any C D E group in the upper part of the piano.

Listen and feel the pulse as your teacher plays the accompaniment below. When you are ready, play C D E. Experiment by playing E D C.

Mix the letters any way you want and make up your own song.

Have fun!

Accompaniment

Flowing (♩ = 85)   🔊 21

Repeat as necessary

With pedal

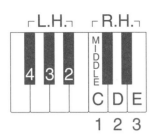

Balloon Ride

Phillip Keveren

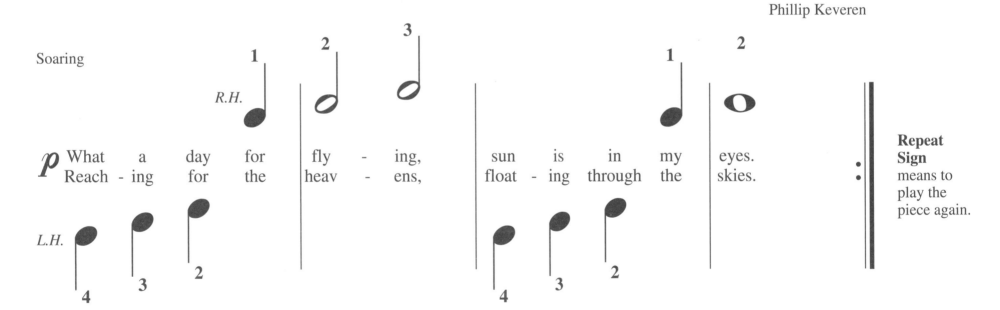

Soaring

R.H.

p What a day for fly - ing, sun is in my eyes.
Reach - ing for the heav - ens, float - ing through the skies.

L.H.

Repeat Sign means to play the piece again.

Hold down the right pedal (damper pedal) throughout.

With accompaniment, student starts here: 🔊 **22/23**

Soaring (♩ = 120)   R.H.

L.H. *p*

24

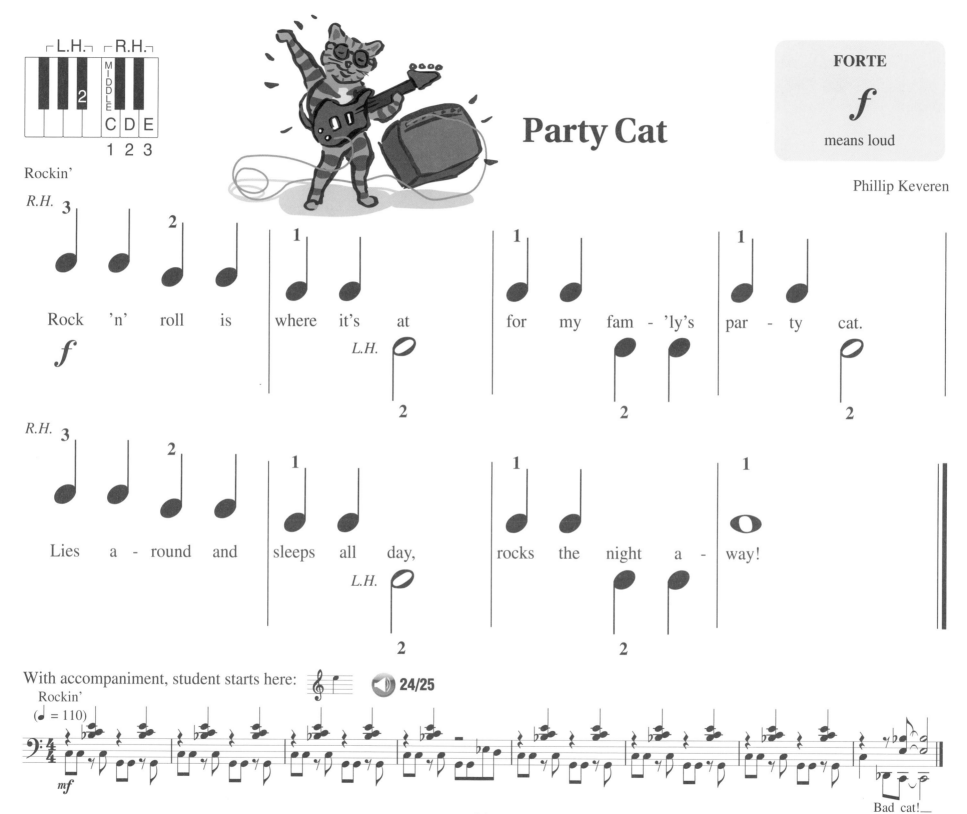

Party Cat

FORTE

f

means loud

Phillip Keveren

Rockin'

R.H.

Rock 'n' roll is | where it's at | for my fam - 'ly's | par - ty cat.

f

L.H.

R.H.

Lies a - round and | sleeps all day, | rocks the night a - | way!

L.H.

With accompaniment, student starts here: 🔊 **24/25**

Rockin'
(♩ = 110)

𝄢 4/4

mf

Bad cat!

F G A B GROUPS

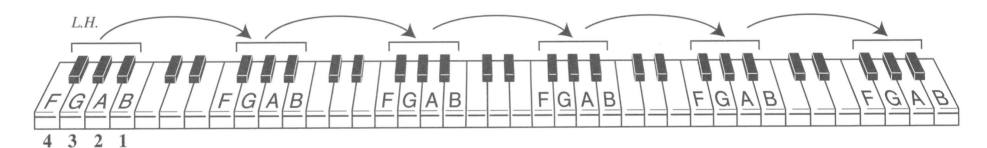

With your left hand, start at the low end of the keyboard and play the
F G A B groups with individual fingers 4-3-2-1 going up the keyboard.

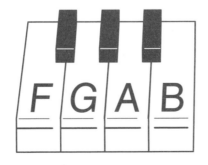

Now explore the keyboard,
playing the F G A B groups
with your right hand using
fingers 1-2-3-4.

My Own Song
On F G A B

With your left or right hand, choose any F G A B group in the upper part of the piano.

Listen and feel the pulse as your teacher plays the accompaniment below. When you are ready, play F G A B. Experiment by playing B A G F.

Mix the letters any way you want and make up your own song.

Have fun!

Accompaniment

Rock beat (♩ = 130)  **26**

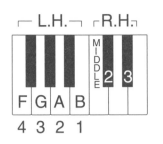

Undersea Voyage

Mysteriously

Phillip Keveren

R.H. **3** **2**

p Deep in - to the o - cean in my sub - ma - rine.
That's the big - gest tur - tle I have ev - er seen!

L.H.

1 **2** **3** **4**

Hold down the damper pedal throughout.

3 **2**

1 **2** **3**

With accompaniment, student starts here: 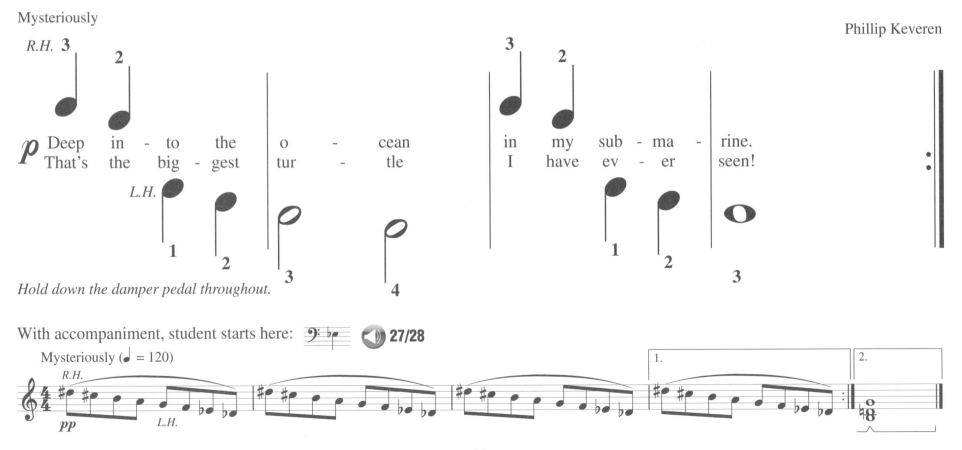 27/28

Mysteriously ($\quad$ = 120)

R.H.

pp *L.H.*

1. 2.

28

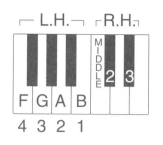

Taxi Tangle

Phillip Keveren

Impatiently

𝆑 Tax - i tan - gle | on the high - way! | Honk! Honk! | Honk! Honk!

L.H. 4 3 2 1 | 4 3 2 1

Skid, bump! 'Xcuse me! | Turned the wrong way! | Honk! Honk! | Honk!

L.H. 4 3 2 1 | 4 3 2 1

With accompaniment, student starts here: 🔊 **29/30**

Impatiently (♩ = 140)

mf

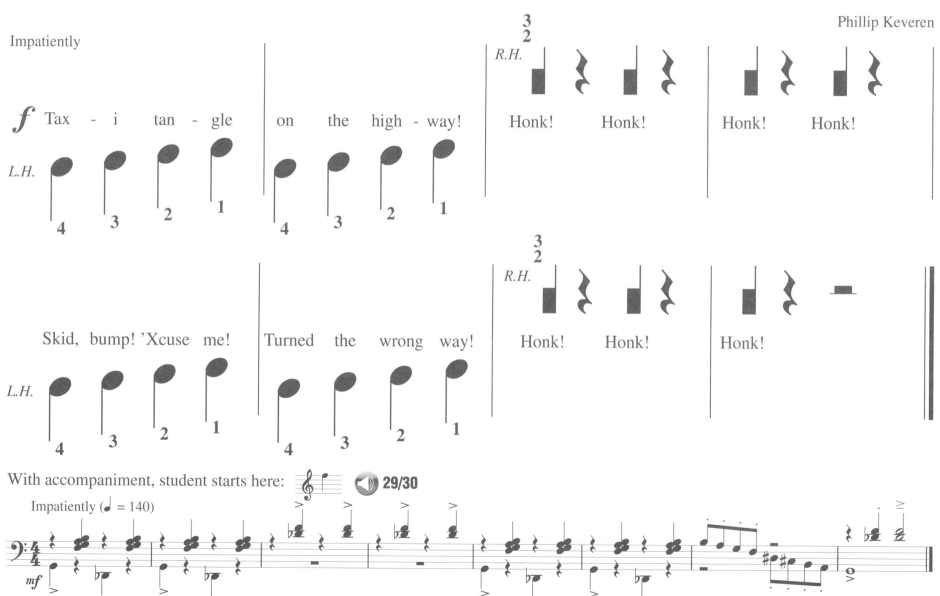

29

TIME SIGNATURE

4/4 (4/4) = four beats fill every measure
= quarter note gets one beat

Count: "1 1 1 1 | 1 1 1 - 2 | 1 - 2 - 3 - 4"
or   "1 2 3 4 | 1 2 3 - 4 | 1 - 2 - 3 - 4"

Sea (C) Song

Fred Kern

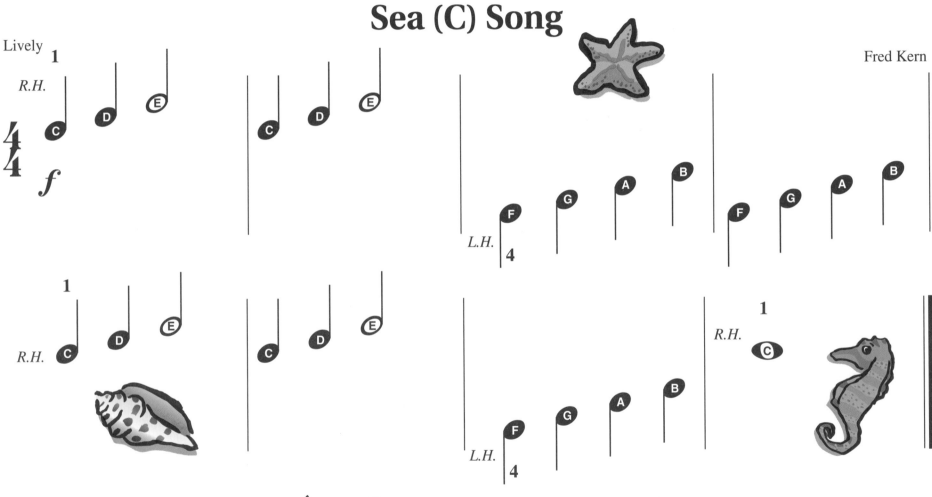

Lively

With accompaniment, student starts here: 🔊 **31/32**

Lively
(♩ = 120)

30

New Position

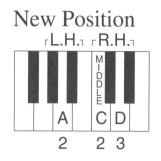

Rain, Rain, Go Away

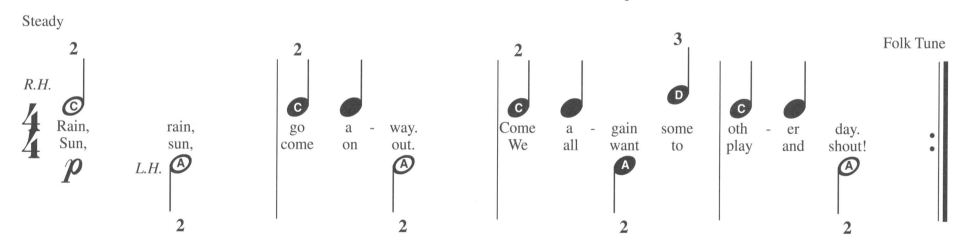

Steady

R.H.

Folk Tune

Rain,   rain,   go   a - way.   Come   a - gain   some   oth -   er   day.
Sun,   sun,   come on   out.   We   all   want   some   to   play and shout!

p

L.H.

With accompaniment, student starts here: 🔊 33/34

Steady (♩ = 120)

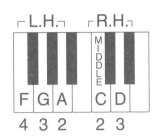

Dakota Melody

Native American

With a steady beat

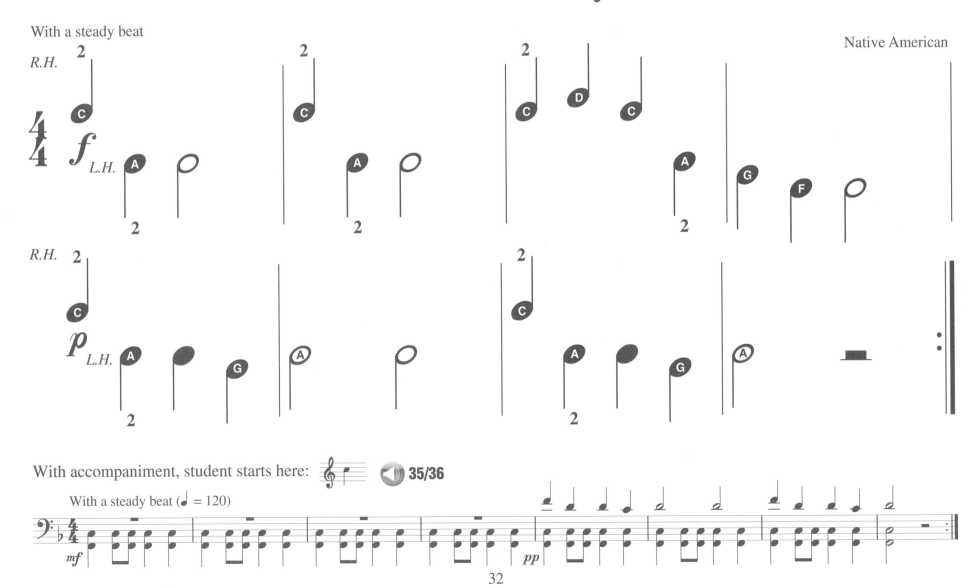

With accompaniment, student starts here: 🔊 35/36

With a steady beat (♩ = 120)

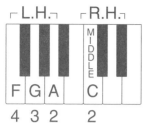

Knock-Knock Joke

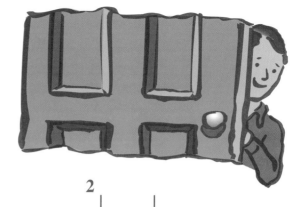

Guatemalan

With humor

Knock on piano cabinet

"Knock - knock."

"Who's there?"

"Knock - knock."

"Who's there?"

With accompaniment, student starts here: 🔊 37/38

With humor

(♩ = 135)

mf

33

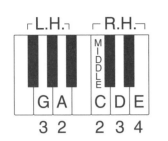

Old MacDonald Had A Band

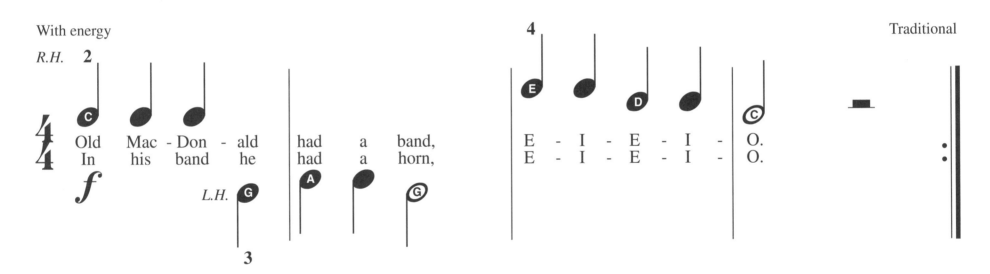

With energy

Traditional

Old Mac-Don-ald had a band, E - I - E - I - O.
In his band he had a horn, E - I - E - I - O.

With accompaniment, student starts here: 🔊 39/40

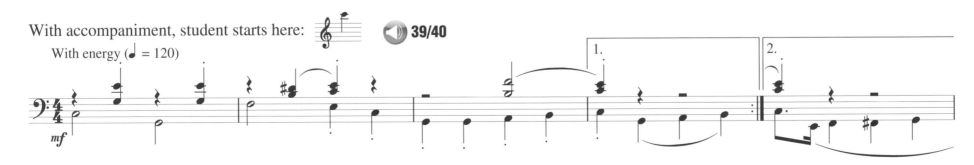

With energy (♩ = 120)

LINES AND SPACES

Some notes are written on **lines:**

LINE NOTE

Some notes are written in **spaces:**

SPACE NOTE

Music is written on a **STAFF** of 5 lines and 4 spaces.

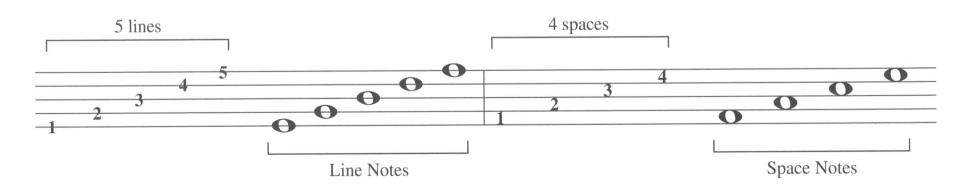

5 lines

4 spaces

Line Notes

Space Notes

HOW NOTES MOVE ON THE STAFF

REPEAT

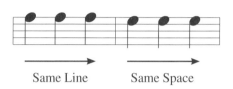

Same Line   Same Space

STEP
(2nd)

Line to Space   or   Space to Line

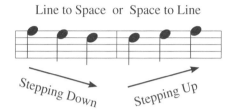

Stepping Down   Stepping Up

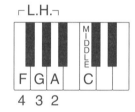

Title:_____

You already know how to play this song.
Do you know its name?

Steady

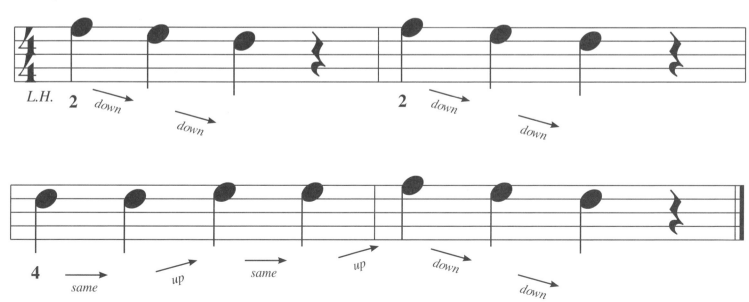

THE BASS CLEF SIGN ∶
(The "F" Clef)

This sign comes from the old-fashioned letter F.

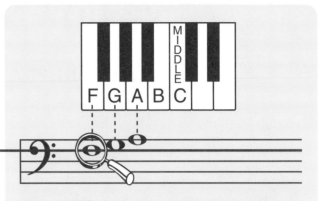

This is the F line _____

The F line passes between
the two dots of the **Bass Clef** sign.

The note F is your reading guide for the Bass Clef. You can name any note on the Bass Staff by moving up or down from the F line.

You will usually play the low tones written
on the Bass Staff with your **left hand**.

Hide And Seek

Mona Rejino

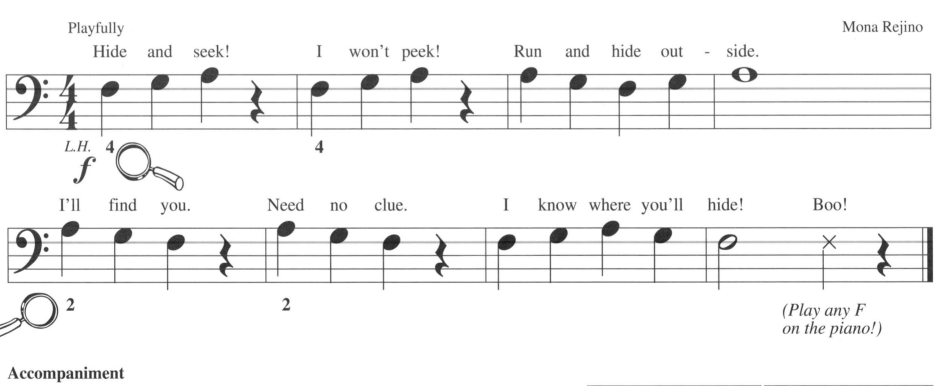

Playfully

Hide and seek! I won't peek! Run and hide out - side.

L.H. **4**   **4**

f

I'll find you. Need no clue. I know where you'll hide! Boo!

2   **2**

*(Play any F
on the piano!)*

Accompaniment

Playfully (♩ = 120) 🔊 **41/42**

mf   1.   2.

8va - - -

38

Whenever you see this magnifying glass, fill in the name of the note.

Title:_____

You already know how to play this song.
Do you know its name?

Bouncy

43/44

L.H. **2**
f

2

39

THE TREBLE CLEF SIGN
(The "G" Clef)

This sign comes from the old-fashioned letter G.

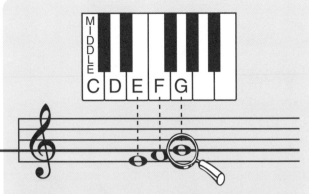

This is the G line.

The G line passes through the curl of the **Treble Clef** sign.

You will usually play the high tones written on the Treble Staff with your **right hand**.

The note G is your reading guide for the Treble Clef. You can name any note on the Treble Staff by moving up or down from the G line.

Oh, Gee (G)

Music by Fred Kern
Words by Claire Berthold

Steady
R.H. 4

Gee, oh, gee. Gee, oh, gee. Four more min-utes, please.

No, not yet. Let us play one more game.

Accompaniment

Steady (♩ = 120)   45/46

40

Hopscotch

Mona Rejino

Bouncy

R.H. 4

f Hop - scotch on the walk. I won - der who will win.

5

2

Lines and spac - es drawn in chalk; now we can be - gin.

Accompaniment

Bouncy ($\bullet$ = 120) 47/48

5

mf

THE GRAND STAFF
A Musical Map

The Bass Staff and the Treble Staff together make the **GRAND STAFF**, a Musical Map that tells you which key to play.

Middle C uses the short line (ledger line) between the Bass Staff and Treble Staff.

Thumbs share Middle C in this position.

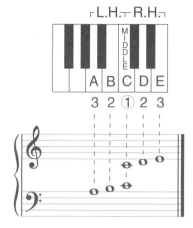

My Best Friend

Happily  49/50

"Pierrot"

f My best friend is *Lind - say. We play ev - 'ry day.*

Hey, we just got start - ed. I wish she could stay.

* Fill in the name of your own friend.

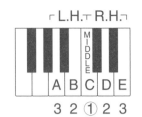

L.H. R.H.

MIDDLE

A B C D E

3 2 ① 2 3

Tambourine Tune

With spirit

1

Folk Tune

f

5

3

1

3

2

Accompaniment (Student plays one octave higher than written.) 🔊 **51/52**

With spirit (♩ = 150)

mf

5

1.

2.

44

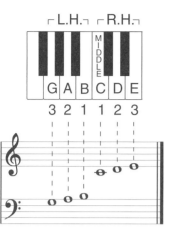

Once A Man Was
So So Mad

Folk Tune

Steady

1. Once a man was so so mad, he jumped in - to a pa - per bag.
2. Pa - per bag, it was so thin, he jumped up - on a point - ed pin.

3. Pointed pin, it was so sharp,
   He jumped upon an Irish harp.

4. Irish harp, it was so pretty,
   He jumped upon a little kitty.

5. Little kitty began to scratch,
   He jumped into a cabbage patch.

6. Cabbage patch, it was so big,
   He jumped upon a big fat pig.

7. Big fat pig began to tickle,
   He jumped upon a big dill pickle.

8. Big dill pickle was so sour,
   He jumped upon a big sunflower.

9. Bee came by and stung his chin, and
   That's the last I've heard of him!

Accompaniment (Student plays one octave higher than written.) 🔊 53/54

45

Long, Long Ago

Thomas Haynes Bailey

Peacefully

mf Tell me the tales that to me were so dear

long, long a - go, *mp* long, long a - go.

Accompaniment (Student plays two octaves higher than written.) 55/56

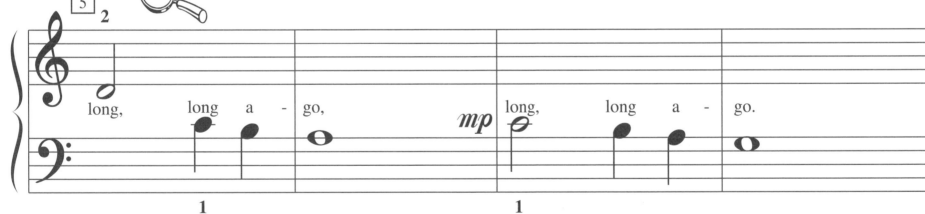

Peacefully (♩ = 120)

mp

p

With pedal

46

MEZZO PIANO

mp

means medium soft

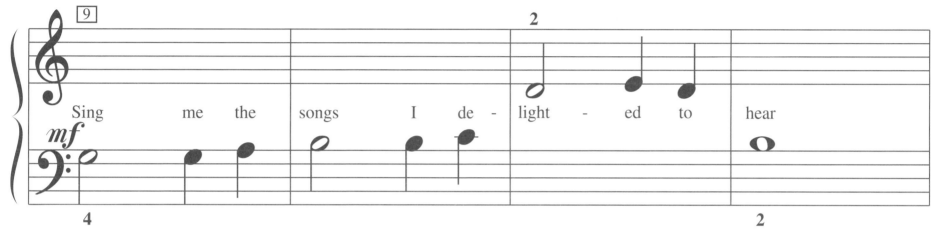

Sing me the songs I de - light - ed to hear long, long a - go, long a - go. *mp*

47

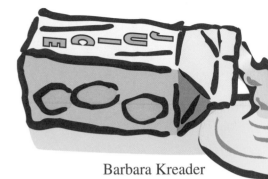

Nobody Knows The Trouble I'm In

Barbara Kreader

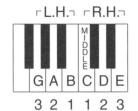

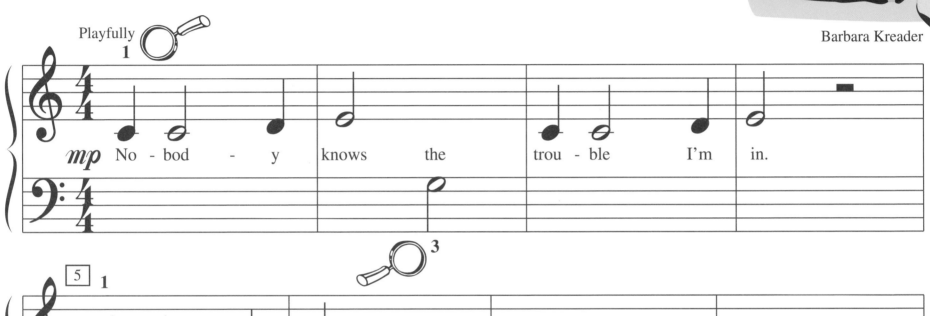

Accompaniment (Student plays one octave higher than written.) 🔊 **57/58**

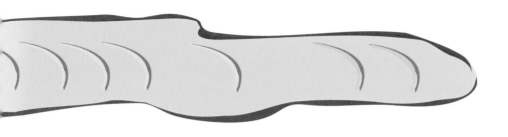

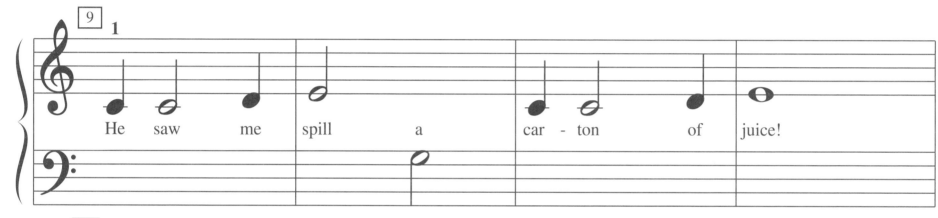

He saw me spill a car - ton of juice!

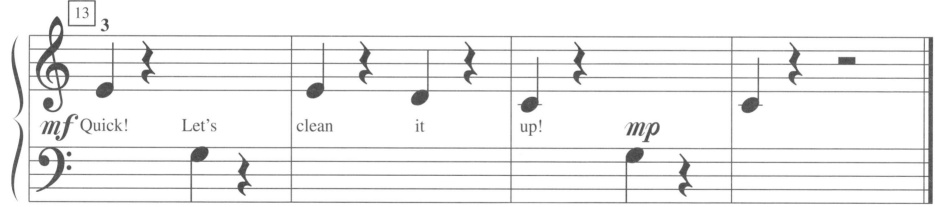

mf Quick! Let's clean it up! *mp*

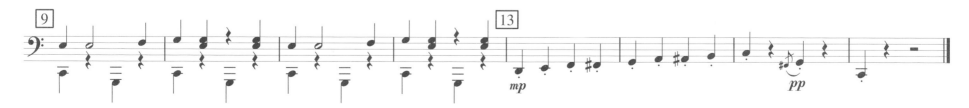

mp

pp

SKIPS
(3rds)

On the Piano, a 3rd
- skips a key
- skips a finger
- skips a letter

On the Staff, a 3rd skips a letter from either
- line to line or
- space to space

Space to Space

Line to Line

Skip down
(3rd)

Skip up
(3rd)

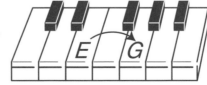

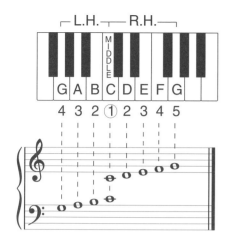

Surprise Symphony

Lively 🔊 59/60

Joseph Haydn
(1732 - 1809)

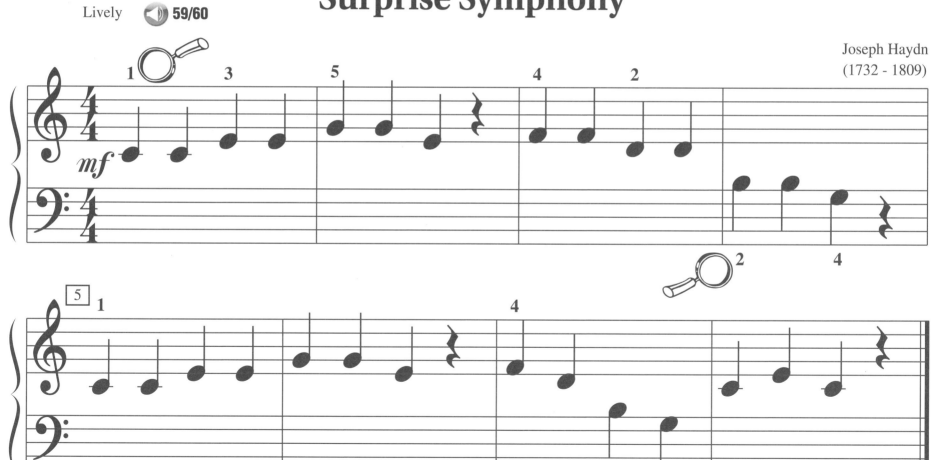

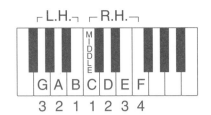

Skateboard Doodle

"Yankee Doodle"

With energy

f Once my broth - er sped down -town, rid - ing on his skate - board.

Took a curve and lost his nerve and turned in -to a trash can.

🔊 61/62

Accompaniment (Student plays one octave higher than written.)

With energy
(♩ = 130)

mf

R.H. over L.H.

8va

Let Me Fly!

Spiritual

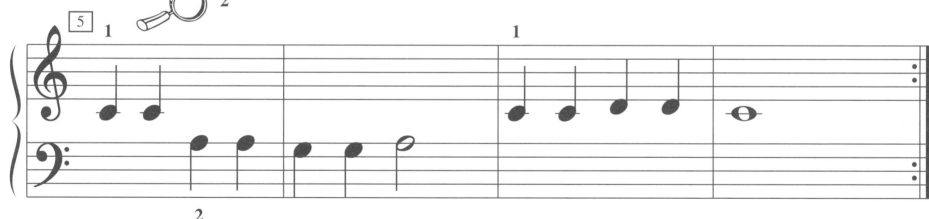

Accompaniment (Student plays one octave higher than written.) 🔊 **63/64**

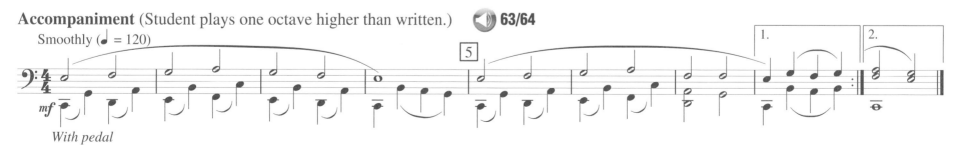

53

Star Quest

Phillip Keveren

Glid - ing through the heav - ens; won - der where we are?

Great ga - lac - tic trav - 'lers, search - ing for a star.

Accompaniment (Student plays one octave higher than written.) 🔊 **65/66**

Heroic March (♩ = 120)

Solemn Event

TEMPO MARKS appear at the beginning of a piece. They tell the mood of the piece and the speed of its musical pulse.

These Italian tempo marks are most common:

	Mood	Speed
Adagio	Seriously	Slowly
Andante	Calmly	Walking Speed
Allegro	Happily	Quickly

Italo Taranta

Accompaniment (Student plays one octave higher than written.) 🔊 **67/68**

55

D.C. (Da Capo) al Fine

When you see this sign, return to the beginning (capo) of the piece and play until you see the sign for the end (fine).

I Like You!

69/70

Allegro

Folk Tune

Fine

mf I like you! You're my own best friend.

Laugh-ing with me when I'm hap-py, stand-ing by me when I'm crab-by,

D.C. al Fine

56

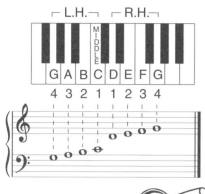

Just Being Me!

Czechoslovakian

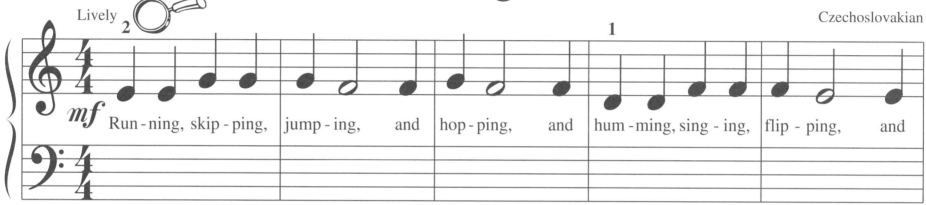

Lively

mf

Run - ning, skip - ping, jump - ing, and hop - ping, and hum - ming, sing - ing, flip - ping, and

flop - ping. I'm hap - py to be *El - lie, I'm El - lie. I'm hap - py to be me!

*Fill in your own name.

Accompaniment (Student plays one octave higher than written.) 71/72

Lively
(♩ = 150)

mp

57

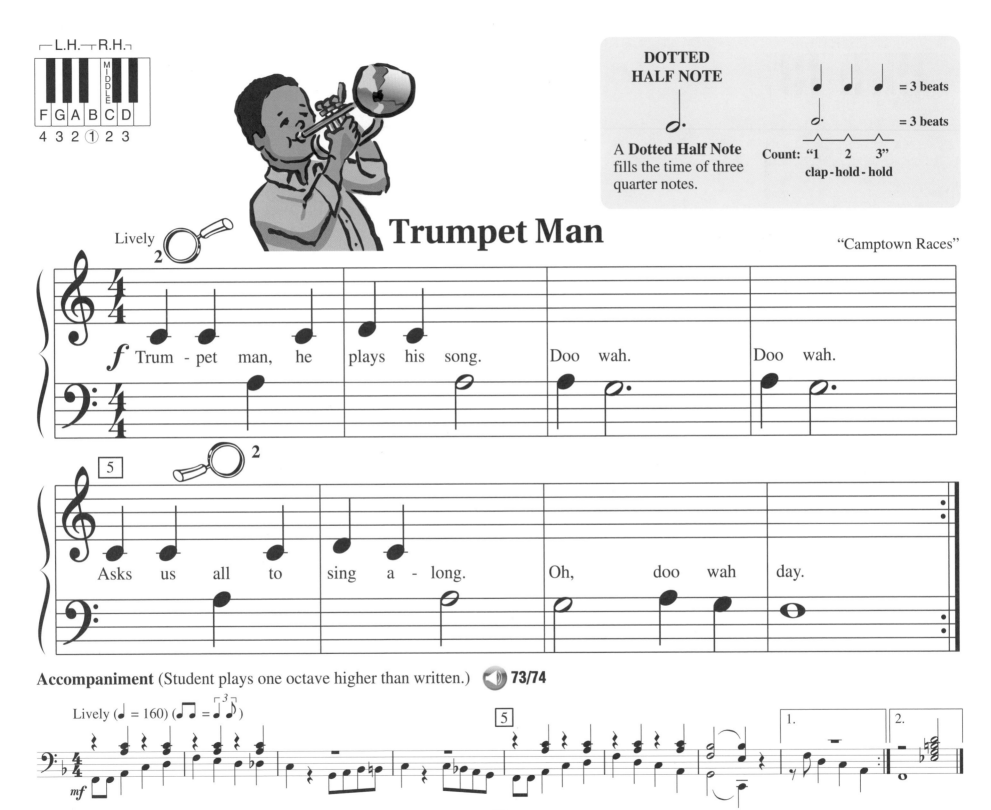

DOTTED HALF NOTE

A **Dotted Half Note** fills the time of three quarter notes.

♩ ♩ ♩ = 3 beats

𝅗𝅥. = 3 beats

Count: "1   2   3"
clap - hold - hold

Trumpet Man

"Camptown Races"

Lively

𝆑 Trum - pet man, he plays his song.   Doo wah.   Doo wah.

Asks us all to sing a - long.   Oh,   doo wah   day.

Accompaniment (Student plays one octave higher than written.) 🔊 **73/74**

Lively (♩ = 160)

58

TIME SIGNATURE

$\frac{3}{4}\left(\substack{3 \\ \text{♩}}\right)$ = three beats fill every measure
= quarter note gets one beat

Scottish Air

Andante — 1

5

Folk Tune

mf Slide   and   step   and   turn   to   the   mu - sic.   The

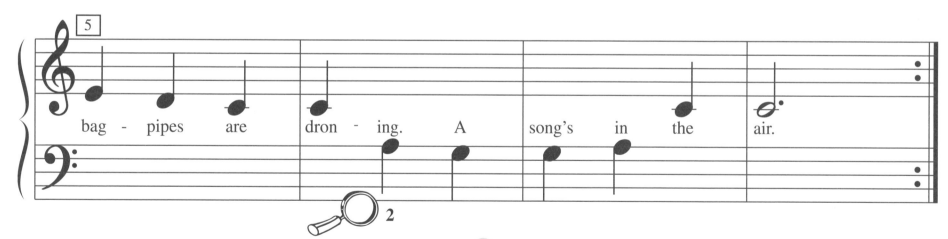

5

bag - pipes   are   dron - ing.   A   song's   in   the   air.

2

Accompaniment (Student plays one octave higher than written.) **75/76**

Andante (♩ = 145)

5

mp

59

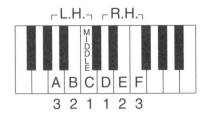

3 2 1 1 2 3

Pirates Of The Sea

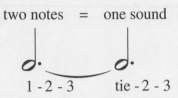

Janet Feldman

Boldly

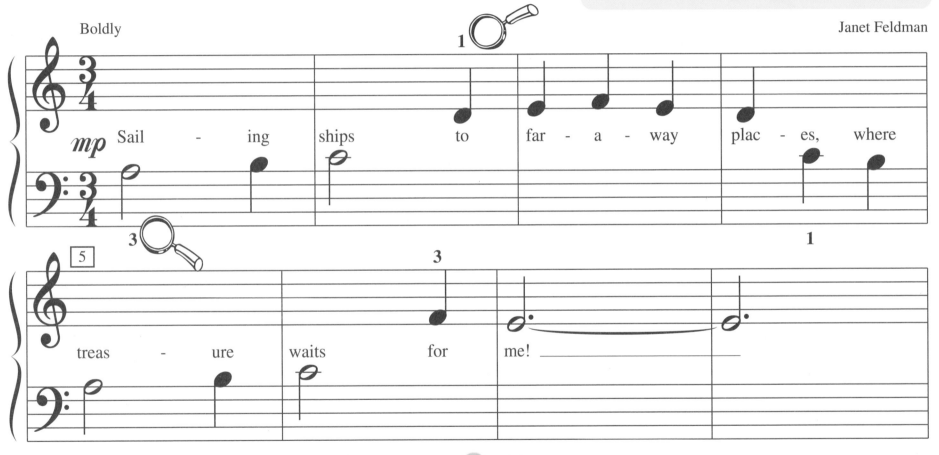

mp Sail - ing ships to far - a - way plac - es, where

treas - ure waits for me!

Accompaniment (Student plays one octave higher than written.) 🔊 **77/78**

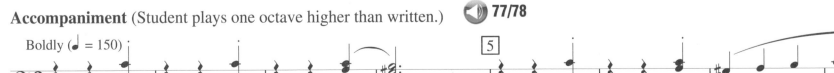

Boldly (♩ = 150)

p

60

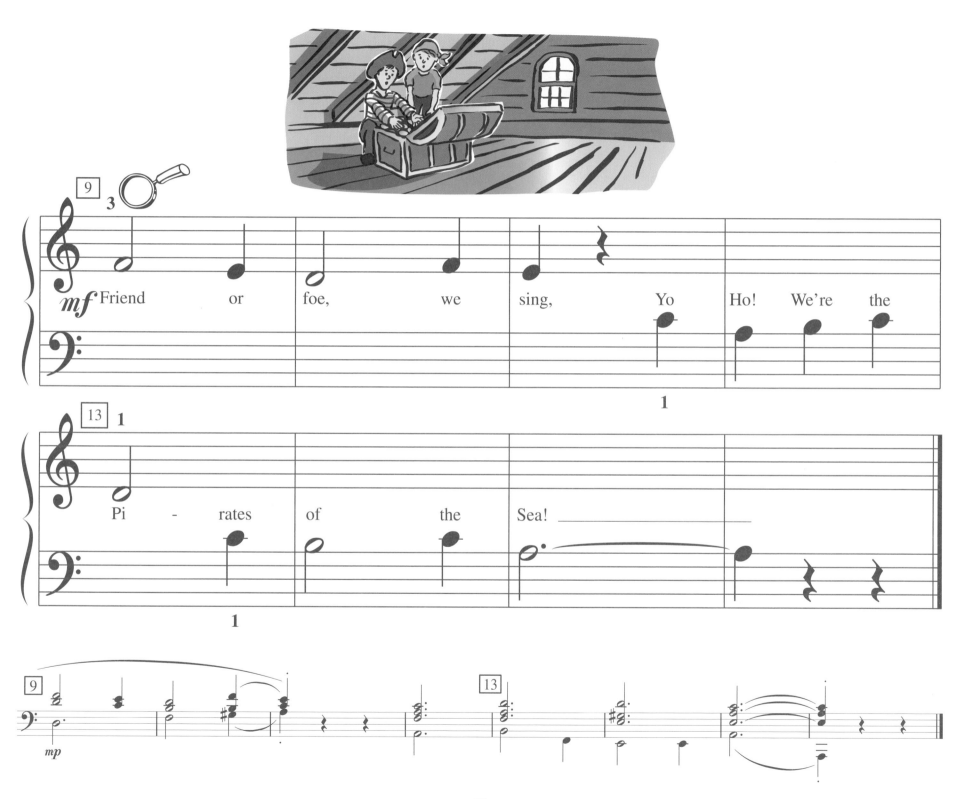

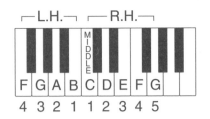

Go For The Gold

Stately March

Phillip Keveren

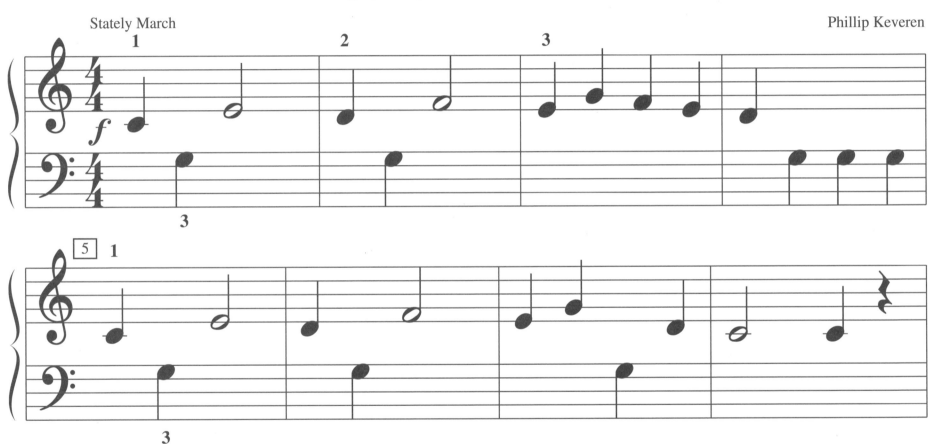

Accompaniment (Student plays one octave higher than written.) 🔊 **79/80**

Stately March (♩ = 90)

AWARD CERTIFICATE

HAS SUCCESSFULLY COMPLETED
HAL LEONARD PIANO LESSONS,
BOOK ONE
AND
IS HEREBY PROMOTED TO
BOOK TWO.

_____ _____
TEACHER   DATE

HAL•LEONARD®

Cut-out may be fitted over student's shirt button.